HAZARDS & HEROES
in
Cornish Mines

Edited by Allen Buckley

For further information of all the titles in this series please visit:-
www.tormark.co.uk

Some of the material in this book was previously published in
Tales of the Cornish Miners. Additional material by Allen Buckley.
All the illustrations are reproduced by kind permission of the Royal
Cornwall Museum, except that on page 37 (G J Nicholas).

Diagram and information boxes by Allen Buckley

Designed by Alix Wood, www.alixwood.co.uk

Published by
Tor Mark, United Downs Ind Est, Redruth, Cornwall TR16 5HY
First published 2007
This reprint 2009

ISBN 978 085025 408 2

Printed by R Booth Ltd, The Praze, Penryn, Cornwall TR10 8AA

HAZARDS
& HEROES
in
Cornish Mines

This schematic diagram of a Cornish tin mine may help you understand some of the special terms used in this book.

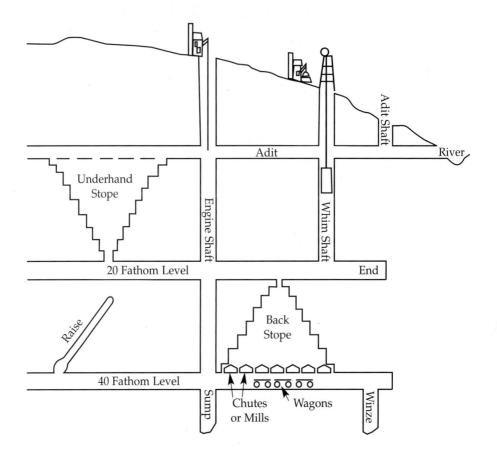

The photographs in this booklet should serve to remind us how conditions underground are intrinsically different from those on the surface. The environment is harsh in the extreme and everything about it tends to make working there hazardous. The rock itself is hard, sharp and unyielding; the almost total darkness; the narrow confined spaces where most miners work, all conspire to make rescue when accidents occur, extremely difficult and dangerous for both the casualty and the rescuers.

HAZARDS AND HEROES
in Cornish Mines

Ever since men first went underground in search of valuable and precious metals, they have faced dangers. Archaeologists testify to evidence of fatal accidents in the mines of the ancient world and no period throughout the Middle Ages was free of such events. An example of this occurred at a Lamorna tin stream in the 1380s, where a miner called Alan Hoskyn was killed when the workings fell in. Richard Carew, who visited west Cornwall tin mines in the 1580s, described the dangers inherent in mining and commented on the type of men who faced them. There has always been danger from poor ventilation, danger from falling rocks, danger from falling off ladders and eventually, when gunpowder was introduced for blasting, danger from premature explosions. The daily risk of accidental injury or death has been accepted by miners throughout history, but if there was one thing which has always reassured them as they went underground to face these dangers, it was their absolute reliance upon the loyalty, selflessness and courage of their mates. Confidence that if things went badly wrong their colleagues would be there to help them, even at the risks to their own lives, sustained these men even in the worst of situations.

In examining some examples of accidents that have occurred in Cornish mines during the last couple of hundred years, it will be noted the great variety of potentially hazardous situations in which miners worked. There is the horrific situation of sudden and devastating water inflow, usually caused by miners breaking into adjacent, flooded mine workings, or by a catastrophic storm. Two of Cornwall's worst mining disasters were caused through this – thirty-nine miners drowned at East Wheal Rose and twenty at Wheal Owles. Exhausted men falling from ladders as they climbed to surface; men maimed, blinded or killed by premature gunpowder explosions; sudden falls of rock in a stope or on the level, were all common accidents throughout the 18th, 19th and 20th centuries. One significant fact can be seen with respect to so many of those accidents: the heroism and unselfishness of the miners who tried to rescue their injured or trapped workmates. This small book seeks to remind us of these men, for they were an integral part of the long and fascinating story of Cornish mining.

Rock Fall & The Dangers of Stoping

Some of the worst accidents in Cornish mines occurred through rocks falling upon miners in stopes. During the last fifty years of its operation South Crofty had eight fatal accidents underground, and five of these were caused by rock falls, mostly in stopes. In May 1977 an accident happened to a miner there, which but for the determination of other miners could have had disastrous consequences. Jimmy Clemence was back-stoping above 340fm level on Dolcoath North Lode, with his mate Dennis Browne. The back was 'blocky' and prone to breaking away and both men

> STOPE: A place from which ore is extracted. Stopes lie between levels and can be worked from below the level (underhand stopes) or from above the level (back stopes). The latter are often called 'shrinkage stopes', because the miner works off the broken ore, which is then pulled through chutes into wagons on the level beneath, thus shrinking the ore in the stope. An empty, worked out stope is called a 'gunnis'.

had spent a long time barring down the loose and dangerous-looking ground. Jimmy described it as: 'Hard and brittle, cracking off all the time. Air blasts all the time!' The lode was fairly flat and varied in width from a metre or so to six or seven metres, although where Jimmy was working it was about three metres wide. When one end of the stope was deemed safe, Jimmy began to drill the benches whilst Dennis continued to bar down. After an hour or two Dennis went for the dynamite whilst Jimmy finished off the drilling. Dennis was back in the stope when quite suddenly and without warning, the roof fell in – right on top of Jimmy Clemence! All his mate could see of him were his feet.

Jimmy Clemence was smashed to the floor of the stope, with his

Holman drill still going. He fell between two large rocks, which partially took the weight of the rockfall and clearly saved his life. As he was flattened his helmet was crushed into his face, causing horrific injuries. His arm, which he had put up instinctively as the rock broke above him, was trapped behind his head. His arm and collar bone were both badly broken. As he lay pinned beneath the rock, which weighed almost a ton, he could not see and thought he had been blinded and that the rock was pushed into his face. Fortunately for Jimmy, his mate, Dennis Browne, was enormously strong. Taking the weight of the rock he screamed for Jimmy to wriggle backwards out from under it, hoping that his mate was still alive and conscious. Jimmy did so, tearing his chest and face very badly. Dennis helped Jimmy to the side of the stope, where they both sat and gazed at the great rock which had fallen. After lighting a cigarette and putting it into Jimmy's mouth, Dennis went for help. Jimmy says that he could not see much, as the skin and flesh of his nose and cheek were flapping about in front of his eye, and blood was streaming from every inch of his face.

All the men on the level rushed to assist in the rescue, with Winston Edwards, a fitter, and Dennis Bray, the shiftboss, helping Jimmy's mate to get him out of the stope and onto the level. Jimmy was carried to New Cooks Kitchen Shaft and taken to surface. Howard Mankee (the mine captain) was there to greet him, and seeing Jimmy's face, and thinking that he had lost an eye along with his other injuries, spoke reassuringly about how a man could manage perfectly well with just one eye. He was horrified when Jimmy reached up with his good hand and flapped the swinging half of his face back into position. He still chuckles as he remembers Howard's look of astonishment! Jimmy Clemence continued mining and was the man who sank South Crofty's second sub-incline to below the 470fm level – on the same horizon as the 550fm level of Dolcoath Mine – the deepest level in Cornwall!

BAR DOWN: Before a miner can begin work at the beginning of a shift he has to ensure that the rock above his head is secure and he can work safely. He and his mate will use high-tensile steel bars to clean or scale any loose or dangerous looking rock from the back or roof of their stope or working place. This safety work is known by the miners as 'baring down'.

After Dennis Browne left Jimmy Clemence he went stoping with Bob Stevens, and whilst working with him he also had a horrific accident. Once again it was a rock fall which caused the accident and once again it was the skill, courage and determination of his mates which saved his life. Dennis was working in a stope between the 290 and 310fm levels, when a rock weighing between ten and fifteen tons came away from the hanging-wall and pinned him to the side of the stope. The training of his rescuers was crucial to getting him safely from a potentially fatal situation. Terry Mankee, John Hendra, Tony Pope and George Curtis, the underground manager, worked tirelessly with the other miners to secure the enormous tonnage of rock threatening them, before removing the part of the rock which held him securely against the wall. The rescue took great self-discipline and courage on the part of the miners working to extricate Dennis, for one false move could have left several dead.

The same training and courage saved the life of David Ellisdon, when he was half buried by a fall of ground as he was putting in place a 'blind cover' over the 310fm level on No 8 Lode. Without regard for their own safety, his mates worked to dig David out before more stuff came down and buried them all.

Rock Crushers & Grizzlys

Twentieth century mines usually had ore passes to send the broken ore to the bottom of the mine, where large rock crushers reduced the ore to a size that could easily be hoisted. Each level would have access to these ore passes and across the top of each ore pass was a grizzly of crossed metal bars through which the trammers would beat the ore with 14lb (6k) sledge hammers. Below 380fm level at South Crofty there was the main crusher, and between the grizzly and the mouth of the crusher, which was some six metres below the level, were large, hydraulically operated metal fingers. When 380fm level was being opened up, in the late 1960s, the shiftboss was Bill Prisk,

Two MACHINE-MEN drilling on 375fm level at Dolcoath, in March 1904. These drifter machines, powered by compressed air, were extremely heavy, some weighing 300lb (136k). They were called bar-and-arm machines because they were supported by vertical bars, which carried a horizontal arm upon which the machine rested. Note, the compressed air powered water spray for damping down the dust. (RCM)

and one day he had a very nasty accident. A teenager, called Geoff Sullivan, was working on 380 Cooks Station, beside the crusher stairway, when above the din of the crusher he heard screaming. Looking down toward the crusher he saw a man's arm protruding from between the hydraulic fingers above the crusher. The crusher operator, who could hear nothing because of the noise from the machinery, was about to open the fingers and send the shiftboss into the mouth of the crusher, where he would have been killed. The youngster stopped the crusher and shouted for the operator to help him. Bill Prisk had been breaking rocks on the grizzly when he slipped and fell through the bars into the ore pass. Sullivan and the other men present had to dig the shiftboss out from beneath the rocks, which had followed him down into the pit. After a heroic and highly dangerous struggle, they succeeded in extricating Bill from his awful situation. When the mine captain, Roy Thomas arrived, he congratulated one of the older miners, who had arrived late for the rescue, and sent him up for an early bath. When Geoff

Sullivan suggested that he might also go up early, as he was exhausted and his fingers were cut to pieces with digging out the rock, the mine captain replied: 'If you couldn't take a joke my son, you shouldn't have joined!' and laughing, he walked off.

Fourteen years later, another man nearly had the same experience. Allen Buckley (editor of this book) and Roy Hooper were mucking the draw-points in Tincroft on Pryces Lode. They were on afternoon shift and at about 8 o'clock in the evening they had just tipped a train of wagons onto the grizzly, and whilst Roy Hooper grabbed a quick cup of tea and a sandwich, Buckley took his turn on the grizzly. He worked his way along the rock pile breaking the ore with his 14lb (6k) sledge. As he stepped onto a large piece of ore, it moved, causing his leg to go down between several large rocks. The crusher man, Vivian Mitchell, was operating the machine six metres below and the noise was terrific. As the rock were drawn down into the pit Buckley found himself being pulled inexorably down with it. He shouted at Roy, whom he could see through the wheels of the wagons only a short distance away, but Roy merely gazed straight ahead, oblivious to his mates's danger. With the situation seeming hopeless and his right leg being almost literally pulled from his body, rescue came from an unexpected direction. Early nightshift started at 8 o'clock and Maurice Shore, a nightshift trammer, had just pulled onto the station to check for wagons when he saw Buckley's predicament. Jumping onto the grizzly he grabbed the large rock which was pulling the man into the pit, and using all his strength, he managed to lever it off the trapped miner. As Buckley dragged himself back onto the grizzly bars he and Maurice looked through the wagon wheels and burst out laughing, as Roy Hooper was still eating his croust and gazing straight ahead, totally unaware of the adjacent drama.

Accidents Through Falling

A major cause of serious accidents in mines has always been through falling. Historically, many fatal accidents happened when exhausted men fell from ladders as they made their weary way to

FATHOM: A fathom is six feet. Fathoms were commonly used as a standard measurement of height and distance in Cornish mines, as well as at sea. Until the 1970s, the miners' contract sheets at South Crofty showed payment in fathoms, feet and inches. Contracts were paid at so much a fathom of ground driven, raised or sunk.

surface. But, there are other reasons why miners fall, and falling down through stopes is one of them. In 1934 a teenager called Jack Jervis was working in an underhand stope with a miner called Mark Hoskin. The stope was below the 290fm level on New Cooks Kitchen side of the mine. Jack worked with Mark in the stope for about eight months when an accident interrupted the youth's mining career. The two miners were clearing loose rock off the point of the bench they intended to drill, when the mine captain arrived and asked to borrow Jack's life-line, whilst he examined some holes they had just drilled. He asked Jack to pass him a long drill and as the youngster stepped onto the loose rock on the point, he slipped and fell some seven metres into the bottom of the stope. Jack lay there, fully conscious, but with a large piece of rock embedded in his skull and his legs and lower body buried by the rocks which had fallen with him. Seventy years later, his skull still has a deep indentation in it. Below Jack was the chute through which the trammers on 310fm level would draw the ore into their wagons. Above him were many tons of broken rock, from their last two blasts, all of it unstable and just hanging there. Jack was in agony from the injuries to his legs, body and his fractured skull, but still aware of what was going on around him, he could see the increasing group of miners looking down into the pit discussing how best to effect his rescue. Just then a miner called Fred Williams arrived with a rope, which he tied off securely, and swung down to the injured boy. Fred had been in the navy during the Great War and appeared unfazed by the dangerous situation he and Jack were in. With little room to move due to the narrowness of the stope bottom, Fred had to work alone to dig Jack out. Finally, after tremendous effort, Jack was released and the men above could begin to slowly haul them both up. Assisted by the men above Fred carried the youth up the side of the stope, with Jack hanging around his neck. Jack Jervis returned to the mine after six months and went to work in South Crofty's tinyard. A year later he went back underground and apart from a few years during the Second World War he continued mining until 1980, when he retired. Jack Jervis spent several years mining in Central and West Africa and is credited with introducing several innovative techniques into the old mine. Fred Williams' heroism was not recognised in any way, he merely went back to his job and regarded it as all part of a miner's life.

In February 1983 there was a dreadful accident in Robinsons Shaft, when the underground manager, George Curtis (chap who'd helped in an earlier accident), fell some 45 metres and survived. Accompanied by Eddie Leak, a mine captain, Curtis was inspecting the shaft, when he saw something which he thought needed closer inspection. Somehow he slipped and fell through the shaft, landing across a timber balk 45 metres below. He lay there very seriously injured and completely unable to move. Over 300 metres below him was the shaft sump. Eddie Leak raised the alarm and set in motion a most extraordinary rescue. Led by Terry Mankee, the mine rescue team swung into action, and despite the desperately dangerous position they were all in, they managed to

PHOTOGRAPH TAKEN IN March 1904 on 375fm level at Dolcoath. The improvised platform on which the three miners are standing to drill a hole, is typical of how miners used whatever was handy to access the place they needed to work. Note, the use of sound ladders and those damaged and discarded, together with an old pipe. The two men in the foreground are mine captains or shift bosses who have accompanied the photographer. The miners have paused for the photograph and the other two are posing. (RCM)

secure the injured man and bring him to safety. This was another case where the skill and training of the rescuers was as important as their personal courage in bringing it to a successful conclusion.

Their courage was more than matched by that of George Curtis, as he fought his way back to health, returning to the mine and even going back underground. Eventually, he went abroad mining and successfully pursued his career despite the horrific injuries he sustained from his accident. A television film was made about the accident in which the extraordinary circumstances were reconstructed.

Death by Gassing

Unlike coal mines, metalliferous mines do not usually have a problem with gas. However, there is one source of gas, which at times has proved dangerous and sometimes even fatal. The gaseous fumes, which are produced by the use of some explosives, have caused problems in many Cornish mines. In the 1930s South Crofty began to use different types of dynamite and some of them had unwanted characteristics. The explosive Victorite was relatively powerful and the miners started to use it for the 'cut' or first part of the round they were blasting. The cheaper and less powerful explosive Burrowite, was then used for the rest of the holes. Burrowite, manufactured by the Burrowite Explosives Company at Trago Mills, had an unfortunate quality – it gave off a large amount of poisonous carbon monoxide gas, which was hard to clear. In September 1937 this gas created a major incident at South Crofty, which was to prove fatal for two of its miners. Stanley Bawden and Charles Smith were engaged in putting up a raise from 290fm level to 260. Bawden was the 'taker' and the 19 year old Smith

was his mate. Smith had worked underground for three years. At the beginning of the shift, Bawden had gone up the ladderway to check that all was in order and the youngster followed him up. Bawden then climbed down the ladder to fix up the water hose so that he could wash the face prior to barring down any loose rock. Bawden shouted up to Smith and upon receiving no answer climbed back up to see what was amiss.

He found his mate unconscious on the rock pile and managed to drag him back to the ladder rearing, but as he was unable to get him down the ladderway unassisted, he went

RAISE or RISE: A raise or rise is an inverted shaft, in that it is mined upward from the level where it begins toward the next level. These raises were to give access and ventilation to stopes and to levels above. Most raises followed the dip of the lode and some were driven at an angle of about forty-five degrees up the dip of the lode and sideways. These flatter raises were considered safer to mine than the steeper ones. Box-holes were short raises which gave access to the stope above a level so that ore could be pulled through the chutes installed in the box-hole.

for help. There followed one of the most extraordinary rescue attempts seen in a Cornish mine. Richard Sedgemore and Jimmy Barnard hurried to the scene,  followed by every miner on the level. Sedgemore and Barnard immediately climbed the ladder to get to Smith, but Barnard fell unconscious from the ladder, sustaining severe injuries to his head and back, whilst Sedgemore pressed on. At the inquest it was said that Richard Sedgemore 'lost his life in a gallant attempt to rescue Smith'. He lay at the top of the ladder rearing, overcome by carbon monoxide gas. Bawden, who had climbed back behind the two men got as far as Sedgemore, whom he spoke to, but he was then overcome by the fumes and retreated to the level, once again.

At this point in the proceedings Captain Tom Williams arrived with two shiftbosses, S Nichols and A Nettle, and they all tried to get to the gassed men, but were driven back by the fumes, which appeared to be getting worse. As they climbed into the gas, Nettles collapsed and fell onto Nichols underneath him, who struggled to get his sick colleague back to the level. Donald Downing and Charles Butler then struggled up the ladder and were overcome by the gas. These were followed by other miners who arrived on the scene and took their turns to attempt to rescue their mates. Eventually, the manager, Clarence Paull insisted that nobody else should try until the air pipe had blown the gas away. Once the manager thought it safe, Butler climbed up to the two dead men and prepared to make them ready for lowering to the level.

As a result of this incident, two miners were dead, three were hospitalised due to carbon monoxide poisoning, one had sustained other serious injuries and ten men were badly affected by the gas, which rendered some of them temporarily blind. Only the prompt use of oxygen by the resident St John's Ambulance man, Superintendent Jory, kept some of the collapsed miners alive. At the inquest Clarence Paull (the mine manager) stated: 'I cannot pay too high a tribute to the heroism displayed by all the men who assisted. Men were dropping all around as the gas reached them. The effect of it was almost instantaneous.' If we attempt to picture the scene at the foot of the ladder, in that narrow tunnel, with injured, sick and semi-conscious miners sitting and lying around, whilst others struggled to get past them to take their turn up the ladder, we can only be astonished at the sheer bravery of those ordinary Cornish miners.

The Terror of Sudden Flooding

Two of the worst accidents in the story of Cornish mining have been caused by flooding. At North and East Wheal Rose in July 1846, some 39 miners were drowned when a violent cloudburst engulfed the mine workings. In January 1893, 20 miners were drowned when the flooded workings of Wheal Drea, which lies next to Wheal Owles, broke into the mine.

The sudden inrush of water which occurred at Wheal Reeth Mine, in January 1937, was not only catastrophic, but it was so very nearly disastrous. The accident happened at 4.30pm on a Saturday, when only a dozen men were still underground. A thin wall of rock between Wheal Reeth and the neighbouring Wheal Boys collapsed, sending torrents of water pouring into Wheal Reeth. Most of the men were working on the deepest levels of the mine, at the 310ft and 220ft levels. As the water burst into Wheal Reeth there was a terrific blast of air and a roaring sound as the water rushed into the mine, causing those miners at the 310 level closest to the shaft to realise that they were in great danger. The miners closest to the shaft immediately began to climb the 90 feet (28 metres) to the 220ft level, unselfishly leaving the cage, which was on 310 station, for the miners they thought would get to the station when they heard the water inrush.

One of these miners, Clifford Bowden, who was in a stope above the 310, also heard it and knew that they were all in danger. Realising that two men, called Weeks and Semmens, were working in the end, and would not be aware of what was happening, he courageously climbed down to the level and went into the end to warn them. As the water was rising rapidly and there was no way back to the shaft, the three men climbed up into a stope, hoping to make their way up to the 220ft level. The stope went only twenty feet above the 310 level, but at the end was a raise which went to the 220 level. Unfortunately, water was cascading through the 220 level and pouring down through the raise to such an extent that there was no way the three miners could climb up through it. Fortunately, after a while the flow slackened, and they heard Semmens' father, a shiftboss, calling from above. A rope was thrown down to them and they attempted to clamber to the 220 level. Weeks and Bowden made it, but in the noise and confusion the younger Semmens lost his grip on the rope and fell back into the stope. Realising what had happened, his father was lowered into the stope where he found his dazed son lying on a pile of ore surrounded

A SCENE OF JOY as three miners who had been trapped underground for two days were rescued from the depths of Wheal Reeth Mine in Breage. The mine was flooded by water from Wheal Boys Mine in January 1937. It took 48 hours to lower the water sufficiently to rescue the three men. Their mates showed extraordinary bravery in locating and rescuing them. (RCM)

by rising water. He undoubtedly saved his son's life. A rescue party was eventually able to get through to them.

While this was going on, three other miners were becoming trapped on the deepest level. David Sedgeman, John Bates and GANP Williams were caught by the speed of the water inrush, and although Bates said he heard a shout: 'Run for your lives!' he had no time to respond. He was hit by a solid wall of water, which almost swept him away. He managed to grab an air pipe and drag himself to the bottom of a raise he could scramble up.

Climbing in total darkness into a stope, he found Sedgeman and Williams. After they had lit a candle they were able to assess their situation, and although they realised that the water seemed to have stopped rising, they knew they were trapped. The three miners began to climb higher in the stope, hoping to stay clear of the water below. There they stayed as the miners, the pump-men, the managers and the Mine Inspector, worked tirelessly to clear the mine of water and make contact with them. As the water was lowered, extremely slowly, miners constantly tried to get through to their trapped work-mates. Several of them waded up to their necks to get through the flooded levels, without success. Eventually, Clifford Bowden once again demonstrated his amazing bravery, by swimming along the flooded level with a flask of hot coffee and an electric torch to make contact. The water was icy and upon his return the courageous man collapsed. Shortly thereafter a dozen miners formed a chain through the neck-deep water to guide the three trapped men to safety.

It is hard to imagine the ordeal these men endured. For fifty hours they waited not knowing when or if they would be rescued in time. They were cold, hungry and mostly in complete darkness. They were probably all wet, but Bates had been engulfed in water, and must have been soaked. The miners told how they sang hymns and prayed that their loved ones would be looked after should they not survive. Sedgeman told reporters that he 'kept up a continual tapping with the men above, and how long we were there I had not the faintest idea. It was a great joy to us when Bowden, who had swum through the tunnel, shouted to us from below.' Once again, it was the miners' comradeship and fearless courage, which brought this near disastrous situation to a happy ending.

A similar accident, but with a less happy result, occurred at North Levant Mine on April 1st 1867. Rarely has there been a more heroic story of danger and escape as that of Ritchie Warren and his son, William, who fought their way through torrents of water in total darkness to escape from certain death. North Levant formed what is now known as Geevor Mine, and alongside it were the abandoned and flooded workings of Wheal Maitland. On that day in 1867, miners stoping above the 70fm level at North Levant broke into Wheal Maitland and released an ocean of water into their mine. Three men were swept along the level, narrowly escaping with their lives. The water fell in vast quantities into the 85fm level, drowning a father and son. It plunged on through winzes and shafts to the 100fm level, where it pulverised the two sons of the resident mine captain.

Ritchie Warren, the mine pitman, who would normally have been working in the Engine Shaft, happened to be working in an end on the 115fm level. He was assisted by his son and a nephew. The three men heard and felt the sudden inrush of water, like a vast, continuing explosion. Realising their danger they set off for the nearest winze, hoping to climb out of danger, but soon found that it was full from side to side with solid water. Their lights gone, and struggling against the enormous weight of water, they forced their way through the winze and set off for the shaft. Before they reached the shaft they realised the nephew was missing. He had just recovered from a severe fever and did not have the strength to fight through the water. At the shaft Ritchie went ahead to try to find where it was best to try to climb up. Feeling around the timbers, in total darkness, with thousands

> WINZE or WINDS: A winze, which was called a 'winds' at Dolcoath, was an internal shaft, sunk between levels for purposes of access and ventilation. In the 17th and 18th centuries, winzes were also important ways of opening up new ore-bearing ground. Many mines were deepened by means of winzes. The origin of the word might be connected to the work 'windlass', as every winze had its broken ore hoisted to the level above by use of a windlass.

A SCENE FROM the 130 foot level of South Condurrow Mine, which became King Edward Mine and was used for training Camborne School of Mines students. Note, how clean and tidy everything is, with the timberman's saw hanging up and the wagon looking as though it has never contained ore. The students were taught how to build a 'Cousin Jack' chute(mill) like the one in the picture, and how to draw the ore from the stope above the level, through the chute into the wagon or tram. The man in the picture was an instructor, a former miner, who helped teach the students practical mining. (RCM)

blocked by a sollar or staging in the shaft, and so they remained uncomfortably and precariously hanging in the shaft above the swirling waters for about two hours before it stopped rising. If a man slipped from his perch he would certainly drown in the shaft, if the man at the top slipped he would almost certainly carry those below him into the water.

After some time, they decided to tie all the cords they had with them together, to help guide them in their descent. When the first went down his candle went out and they knew the air was bad. They lit another candle and checked again until the air seemed better and as the water had subsided somewhat, they all descended to the tunnel. They then proceeded along the crosscut to the County Adit. When they got there, they placed boards across the main adit to divert some of the water into the shaft they had climbed down, thus lowering the depth of the water and allowing them to get to the footway shaft and make their escape to surface. Surprising as it may seem, this type of danger was a normal hazard for those engaged in checking and maintaining the hundreds of miles of adit tunnels in Cornwall. The quiet almost stoical patience

of those four miners was also typical of the men who carried out such dangerous tasks in the Cornish tin and copper mines.

Trapped in a West Cornwall Adit

The story of another incredible escape from almost certain death in one of Cornwall's ancient adit tunnels was related in the *People's Magazine* in 1872. It was told to them by an old miner, who related a catalogue of horror stories about the dangers of metalliferous mining, including one which was quite terrifying.

'This adit were about a mile long, and as there was some sort of obstruction in it, the captain of the mine ordered one of us to find

SOLLAR: Sollar is a Cornish word for a floor. In mining parlance a sollar can mean a staging or platform in a shaft or internal ladderway, or it can refer to a false floor which facilitated ventilation in a dead end. A circuit would be formed by having the level furthest from the end blocked off, causing the air coming down a shaft or winze to move toward the end and back beneath the floor sollar.

out what it was, and remove it. It fell to the lot of Will Thomas to do this, and several of us saw him enter; but expecting he would go right through to the shaft and out by the ladders, we thought no more about it till, leaving the mine myself some hours afterwards, I saw his young wife standing at the door with her baby in her arms. A stopped to speak a civil word and she asked me if I hadn't seen her Will, and what were keeping him so long.

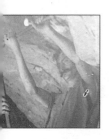 I don't know whether it was her anxious look that made me feel uneasy for a moment, though I answered cheerfully enough that he weren't far behind, and then went on toward my own cottage. But the queer feeling was on me still, and I turned back to meet my mates and ast 'Who's seen Will Thomas?'

No one had seen him since he entered the adit. 'Maybe he stopped at Ludgvan, to have a chat with Dave Pentreath' somebody suggested, and I went home better satisfied, for Dave was a bit of a kin to Thomas, and as he were a wise old man, it was natural that Will should give him a look in every now and then.

Some two hours after this, when I'd almost forgotten all about it, Will Thomas's wife came to the door pale and frightened. He had not returned. Where could he be? Could no one, no one, tell her?

In a moment the thought came across me, 'He's fast in the adit', and blaming myself for not thinking this sooner, I went as fast as my legs would carry me to hunt up all those who had worked in the same core as Will. I offered to be the one to search for him. We miners are used to groping in the depths of the earth, and this was no worse than I had done before, yet my heart beat fast, and the big drops o' sweat stood on my face as I crawled along expecting every moment to come upon the dead body of Will Thomas. Once, though I'm no coward, I was a'most ready to go back. I didn't though, and every odd while I called out to the missing man. But the shout awoke no answer, except the trickling of the little stream that ran along the bottom of the adit, and the echo of my own voice that sounded strangely hollow in my ear.

I'd crawled about a third of a mile, when far away I heard a muffled shriek. Though I had been listening for some sound to

The man-engine at Dolcoath Mine. Introduced into Cornwall at Tresavean Mine, in 1842. The first man-engine to be installed at Dolcoath was working by November 1854. The single rod of the engine moved up and down the shaft at a fairly moderate speed, enabling the miners to safely move from the platform in the shaft onto the step on the rod and off again when the rod paused. At Dolcoath the platforms ('sollars') were spacious and the angle of the rod made riding the man-engine easy. Note, the great width of the lode through which the shaft has been sunk. One of the wheels which carried the rod can also be seen, as can the signal or 'knocker line'. The ladders were there for those who preferred to climb and for use when the engine was not working. Unfortunately, many associate the man-engine with the dreadful accident at Levant, in 1919, when the engine there collapsed, killing 31 men and boys. However, Cornish man-engines saved many hundred lives directly, and lengthened the lives of thousands of miners. (RCM)

27

tell me that Will was still living, a cold shiver ran through me when that dismal screech pealed along the adit; but I shouted back lustily that help were near, and crawled on faster than before. By and by I heard a deep groan, and knew I was nearing the place where he must be. At last, squeezing myself through the narrowest part of the passage, I came to where he lay, wedged in by a slip of the earth.

Pinned down on his face – obliged to throw back his head, which was all he could move, to keep the waters of the stream from entering his mouth and drowning him – you must guess what he was suffering. Seeing the agony he must be in – keeping his head in that position – I took off my coat, and rolling it up, placed it under his chin. Then getting some brandy down his throat, I bade him cheer up while I went back to the shaft for more help.

He gave a gasp, and pitifully begged me not to leave him. I couldn't wonder that he felt as if it were more than he could bear to see me and my lantern go away from him, and leave him once more alone. But there was no help for it, and when I told him it were the only chance of saving him, he said. 'Go, then, Jack, and God bless ee!'

And so I went, but with a sinking heart, for I knowed he were hopeless, and so were I; for it was no easy task to work at a load of earth in a narrow tunnel, and remove it before the fellow underneath were exhausted. But we went to work steadily, every-one eager to take their turn.

It were late next day before we brought Will Thomas out of the mine shaft, and them that stood about it said he were dead. But they were wrong. It were many hours before he  came to, and knew his wife that was watching over him; and it were a long time before he took his spell of work with us again; but he did get well; and maybe he's none the worse now for the time when he lay some twenty hours or more fast in an adit.'

The horror of Will Thomas' situation is almost too dreadful to imagine, but his resigned patience as he waited for his mates to come for him, bears testimony to the confident reliance that miners have in their workmates.

Fire

Fire is a hazard associated mainly with collieries rather than metalliferous mines; for in the latter minerals of a combustible nature are seldom found. However, the extensive use of timber for roof supports and pitwork involved the introduction of a definite fire hazard, particularly where the workings were dry and there was a good draught.

Several spectacular conflagrations have occurred in Cornish mines through the timbers catching alight. One of the most interesting of these involved the destruction of the Great Carbona at St Ives Consols around the year 1844. This carbona, representing one of the most remarkable deposits of tin ever known in

A SCENE TYPICAL of almost any Cornish mine between 1850 and 1960. A young miner is pushing ('hand tramming') a 16cwt (815k), side-tipping wagon or tram along a level. The level is heavily timbered with what were called at Geevor 'square sets' and at South Crofty, 'caps and legs'. (RCM)

Cornwall, branched off at the 77 fathom level, the workings being excavated in enormous caverns 10 or 12 fathoms high and equally wide. Local tradition says that this Great Carbona was as large as St Ives Wesleyan Chapel - itself the largest building in the town.

It proved to be a veritable treasure-house of tin but the rich store of mineral wealth was never fully extracted. A workman left a lighted candle stuck to the roof timbers in the entrance passage; this burnt down, igniting the woodwork, and the flames were communicated to the great stull (made of the largest timber procurable) that supported  the sides and roof of the Great Carbona itself. The fire lasted six weeks and ruined the entire section; but after the flames had subsided, one of the miners, called Nankervis, ventured within and retrieved a fragment of ore which had actually been smelted on one side by the intense heat.

Falls of ground made it impossible to re-work the Great Carbona from below; but years later some miners attempted to sink a new shaft from a position immediately above. Lack of funds, however, prevented the enterprise being carried to a successfull conclusion. The site of the shaft is still pointed out in a croft near Penbeagle Hill. No risk of life was involved in this case; but a similar fire at Dolcoath on 8 January 1890 nearly ended in tragedy. Here, a conflagration broke out in some old stulls over the 235 level near the man-engine shaft, caused, it was believed, by a miner carelessly throwing a lighted candle among them. The night-shift men in the 300 fathom level were driven from their posts by huge volumes of smoke and being unable to ascend by the man-engine shaft had to escape by the new Eastern Shaft, which was ventilated by a downward current.

On the following day the quantity of smoke reaching the surface had not lessened, and all work underground in the centre of the mine had to be suspended. Although there was no danger of the blaze spreading to the main parts of the workings, the management felt some anxiety for the security of the man-engine. Accordingly, two shaftmen called Trevarthen and Weekes descended to the 80 plot and there began to screw down the pole to prevent the plunger from taking air. Trevarthen, however succumbed to the smoke and fumes. and fell to the ground. Three times his companion lifted him to his feet, but ultimately found his own strength failing and they fell to the ground together. Eventually both men became unconscious and remained so for five hours. Two other shaftmen, called Sowden and Wake, who went below with them, managed to get away from the danger area and reached the Eastern Shaft without being overcome.

Meanwhile, at surface, considerable anxiety was felt for the safety of these four men. Several rescuers went down by the new Eastern Shaft to search for them, and the skip was lowered with a signal bell. On the skip being returned, it was found to contain two jackets, showing that two of them at least still lived. A timberman called Semmens and another man who went down in search of Wake and Sowden walked in the direction of man-engine shaft until both became overpowered by smoke and fell to the ground. With their remaining strength and supporting each other, they crawled backwards and on

reaching the gig found to their joy that Wake and Sowden had also arrived there from another level. All four were then drawn to the surface together.

The skip was lowered and raised again and again without further success whilst the anxious watchers at surface waited in a downpour of rain for any sign of the other missing shaftmen. Eventually a miner named Eva expressed the opinion that they were in the 80 plot, and volunteered to go down in the skip if anyone would accompany him. John Rule, brother-in-law to Trevarthen, offered to go, and the two men were lowered into the shaft. Eva's surmise proved

EXPLOSIVES: The first explosive material to be used in Cornish mines was gunpowder or black powder. This was introduced in the 1680s and soon was being used in all Cornish mining districts. By the end of the 19th century high explosives were being used and dynamite especially became the explosive of choice in Cornish mines. Gunpowder was still used in some mines until the 1930s. By the 1970s ANFO (Ammonium Nitrate Fuel Oil) was being introduced and by the 1990s it had largely replaced the use of dynamite.

correct, for they found Weekes and Trevarthen lying on their faces in the 80 plot, still locked in each other's arms. When brought to the surface they were still insensible, and few thought they would recover. Although Trevarthen's mind proved to be temporarily unhinged by the experience he had undergone, both survived their fearful ordeal.

Children in the Mines

Children working or playing on mines, where gunpowder was frequently unsecured and machinery unprotected, have always been in danger. Until recent times little attention was given to such things. The result of this has been some

A COMPRESSED-AIR winch on the 406fm level at Chappels Shaft in Cooks Kitchen Mine, in 1893. Note, the angle of the skip road (left foreground) and the pump column, which conform to the dip of the lode down which the shaft was sunk. The small winze-kibble has just been hoisted from the sump, immediately below the level, where the shaft sinkers were deepening the shaft. The kibble is about to be tipped into the waiting 10cwt (509k) wagon. The patient trammer is standing with arms folded. A fitter is tightening a nut and bolt on the compressed-air line to the shaft sinkers. (RCM)

horrific accidents, which have resulted in many avoidable deaths. One such occurred in June 1868 at Dolcoath Mine.

The miners at Dolcoath kept their gunpowder in lockers in an open shed with a roof but no walls. They were issued with their powder on a Monday morning, in lots of between 10lb and 50lb (4-22k). Although the lockers had keys, there was always gunpowder on the floor of the shed, where the miners had spilled it as they took it to their lockers. Unfortunately, the local children knew of this, and it was a regular practice for boys to gather the powder up to make fireworks with. On June 20th 1868, a 13 year old girl called Fanny Walter, accompanied by her three little brothers, James, Augustus and Alfred, went from Roskear Field, where the Walters lived, to get water from the well at Pengegon Coomb. As soon as the boys were in sight of the powder house, they left their sister and joined three other lads who were going into the locker shed.

The six little boys gathered up some gunpowder in the locker room, and when Fanny saw what they were doing she shouted for them to come away, but it was too late. One of the other boys struck a match on the side of one of the powder lockers and gave it to James to put it into the pile of gunpowder. He did so, and as the older boy and Fanny ran outside there was an enormous explosion. Not only the powder on the floor went up, but each of the lockers in turn exploded, throwing the children about and turning them into human torches. Fanny ran back and grabbed one of her little brothers, who was on fire, and attempted to carry him out of the area, but he was too heavy and she struggled to move him. Despite the efforts of people who ran to help, four of the children were so badly burned that they died. Their ages were 9,7,7 and 5 years old.

At the subsequent inquest various recommendations were made, which, as this was not an isolated incident, was not surprising. It was suggested that in future powder sheds should be more secure, with walls and proper gates. However, no recommendation was made about keeping the powder house floor swept clean of spilt gunpowder. The bravery of the would-be rescuers would also have been noted, especially that of little Fanny Walter.

Some accidents to children happened to those youngsters who worked on the mines. During the summer of 1868 several boys who worked on the dressing floors of Dolcoath began taking their food on the wooden roofs of the sheds they worked in. This practice, typical of boys in every generation, was against the mine rules, and some were warned to stop it and fined, as it was dangerous and damaged the roofs. Undeterred some lads continued with the practice, and in April 1869 it had disastrous results. An eight year old boy, James Eva, had climbed onto the roof at 12 o'clock to eat his croust, in the sunshine. Close by was the revolving rod of some of the tin mill machinery, and the place where James chose to sit on the roof was perilously close to it. At about 12.30pm one of the workers noticed the machinery had stopped working, and glancing up he saw the boy's body wrapped around the rod. James Eva's loose clothes had caught on the revolving rod and he was unable to pull himself clear. The poor lad had suffered a most horrific death.

It was not only little children working on the mines who took risks, for teenager bal maidens were also known to. In July 1873, at Ding Dong Mine, high on the moorlands of West Penwith, two young bal maids stopped work for their mid-day break. One of them, Alice Ann Stevens, set off to get water from a nearby stream, whilst the other, Eliza Jane Hall, climbed onto the big crown gear wheel of the steam winding engine, which was not in motion. Alice shouted to her friend to get off of it, because it was dangerous. Eliza listened to the advice, but then the bell rang and the engine began working. Ignoring Alice's second warning, Eliza climbed back onto the wheel shouting, 'I will go round!'

The wheel went round like a roundabout, and Eliza must have thought it would be fun to ride it, but it was also extremely dangerous. The girl's clothes caught in the gearing and she was dragged to the ground screaming. Hearing this the whim-driver

immediately stopped the engine, but it was too late, for Eliza's body lay torn almost to pieces, with some parts tangled in the machinery and some on the ground. Despite prompt medical assistance it was quite impossible for her to survive and she died a few hours later.

The Wheal Agar skip disaster

One of the Worst disasters known in Cornish mining history took place in Wheal Agar at Pool, on 15 August 1883. An overladen cage was being drawn up the shaft by the steam whim and had just reached the landing place at the top when the wire rope snapped, causing the vehicle to hurtle back down the shaft, killing all twelve miners inside. Only one man, by the greatest luck, managed to spring off in the nick of time before it began its headlong descent to destruction, so saving his life.

The cage was made of iron, divided into two compartments, one above the other. It appears to have been a rather small affair, as the men in the lower compartment could not stand comfortably. There was an opening on two sides, with a bar in the centre, to which the men clung. John Long, the lander, described what happened in these words:

'One set of men who had gone down 'last core at night' had been brought to the surface and safely landed; and when the accident took place a second set of men were in the cage. This had got to 2½ feet above the landing step - that is, the top of the cage. The lip was not put down for the gig. (This lip was a piece of iron which was thrown back to rest the skip upon when it reached surface). 'I had made a token to the whim-driver of the near approach of the cage and I had the rope in my hand about to ring stop. The cage was slowly ascending now, and I heard something going. I had before just caught sight of the heads of the miners in the upper portion of the cage and I glanced up to see what was the matter. At the same moment, one of the men, I cannot tell his name, said, 'What's that going overhead?' I perceived that the rope was parting, and I dropped the ringing rope.

Carbines was on the top of the cage, and he sprang off, and at the same moment the cage rapidly disappeared. I looked over into the shaft, and heard the men give a despairing cry as the cage went out of view. I was so frightened that I felt my blood almost turn to water'.

A search party was immediately organised. They found that the cage had left the skip-road at the 70 fathom level, and from there to the 110 the eastern side of the road was ripped up. At the 110 one body was found. At this place the cage again got into the road, and came to a standstill at the 130, where it ran into the 'plot' and turned over. Two bodies were picked up here. The velocity and alteration of the position of the cage threw the remainder of the men into the shaft. Two were discovered at the 135, two at the 205, and two at the 225. In all cases the condition of the bodies was terrible.

Mr Frecheville, the Government Inspector, later found that the rope used on this occasion was the capstan rope generally employed for pitwork purposes. It was an old one and ought never to have been used for drawing men. The gig had also been grossly overloaded. Only eight men should have been carried at one time, but ten persons were inside, with three more riding on top. This practice of riding on top of the skip was particularly dangerous. At East Pool on one occasion, a man was in such a position when the skip was run to the top of the shears that he was literally bent double; while another miner once had his head cut off by this on a skip at Pendarves United.

Whilst the Wheal Agar accident was clearly attributed to the condition of the wire rope, its terrible consequences could still have been avoided had the cage been fitted with safety catches, which would automatically come into action in the event of the rope's breaking. Previous accidents in Cornish mines had shown how necessary such devices were. At North Basset the rope snapped when three men were being drawn to surface; the cage fell more than 200 fathoms and two of them were killed, the third having an extraordinary escape. Despite such occurrences, the county lagged far behind other mining areas in the provision of safety devices on skips. The Wheal Agar disaster undoubtedly played its part in awakening opinion to the need to safeguard men's lives when using underground winding equipment.

A COUPLE OF timbermen at South Crofty Mine in 1956. They are extending a stope rearing, whereby the ladderway, from which they are working, is protected from the broken ore in the stope. A rearing was a sort of vertical wooden fence, installed alongside a ladderway to separate it from the broken ore in the stope. As the back stope was mined upwards the rearing and ladderway would also be extended. (G J Nicholas)

A miraculous escape

Many hairbreadth escapes from death are recorded in the annals of Cornish mining, but perhaps none more remarkable than one which occurred at Botallack mine, on the cliffs of St Just, in the autumn of 1838. Three men engaged in enlarging the Crowns Engine Shaft had prepared two holes for blasting. Two of the party, Nicholas Bowen and James Grenfell, junior, retreated into a level about six fathoms higher up, leaving James Grenfell, senior, to fire the fuses and follow. Having lit them, Grenfell hastily began to follow his companions to their place of safety. As he reached the top of the ladder leading to the level, it gave way, and he fell to a point a few feet below the burning fuses. The ladder itself dropped into the sump, so that his retreat was completely cut off, and nothing but a mangled and miserable death seemed to await him.

By the light of the fuses he discovered the lift of pumps through which water was drawn up the shaft. Though it seemed a forlorn hope, he clung desperately to this pump and waited for his fate, thinking the while about his five young children and crippled wife. All was darkness save the hissing fuses just above him. The thundering explosion soon followed; but, miraculously, he found himself still alive and breathing. However, his ordeal was not yet over; for through the gloom he saw fire spouting from the other fuse. The second explosion filled the confined space with noise, dust and smoke; but again Grenfell found himself safe, though almost covered in pieces of rock, deaf and speechless, and still clinging to the pump.

His son afterwards described his own feelings at this time in the characteristic St Just dialect:

When I heerd faethur screech, and he and the ladder fale away I knowed 'twas all ovvur; he must, thoft I, be kill'd in one of these here three ways - Ef he's gone to bottom, every lem es brock. - Ef ennything like life es left, he must be drown'd in the sump; and ef he shud be catch'd up by the stage where we belong (i.e. the stage where they stood to work, and which they had just left) the two holes must blow un into a thousand pieces. – Oh, dear! Oh, dear! I faeld down pon my knees, and all that I cud pray was Oh, Nicky, pray for faethur.

Nicky kneeled down, but he dedn't pray, I reckon, for when the holes went off, he said – 'He's out of pain or he's in the sump swemming.'

My lighted candle was on my hatcap; – I catch'd hould ov the lift, slider'd away from flanch to flanch, and was down pon the stope like lightning.

The place was full of smok, and not a lem nor nothing human cud be seed. At laest up agenst the lift I seed faethur's head and shoulders.

The attle was to his brist, and hes face in a dismal shape; hes eyes was uppun, but he cudn't speak. – O, help me, Nicky; help me, doey, to clear away the traed from faethur.

He's glazing, said Nicky, but he caen't be alive, you know; twud kill a thowsand cats ef they'd ben there. – Oh, clear away quicker! quicker! Nicky!

As they frantically strove to remove the rubbish, the lips of the buried man quivered slightly. 'I believe I'm saved, Jimmy, and I baen't hurt much, I reckon, Jimmy', he muttered feebly, to the great joy of his son. Frantically they cleared away the attle, and at last brought the older man out – 'as deef as a haddick; but that and a few smale cuts es awl the hurt that's dun to un'.

A frightful boiler explosion

Mining has always been regarded as one of the most dangerous occupations. Rock falls, premature explosions, falls of ground, flooding, and skip and ladder accidents have all taken severe toll of our Cornish miners. Nor were these accidents confined to underground workers. The primitive, unprotected machinery used on the dressing floors in olden days caused many fatalities and injuries; perhaps the greatest danger of all 'at grass' lay in the boiler houses of the pumping engines. These boilers, often inadequately maintained by the mine engineers and insufficiently supervised by the enginemen, not infrequently blew up with disastrous consequences to anyone in the building.

The only sufferer in most of these explosions was the

engineman on duty; but it sometimes happened that many others were involved as well. This arose from the fact that proper changing rooms were not formerly provided for the underground miners, who consequently had to wash and change their clothes 'over the boiler' attached to the main pumping engine. If an explosion occurred while they were in the building, the number of resultant casualties could he high.

The worst explosion of this kind on record occurred at the United Hills Mine, near Porthtowan in February 1830. The disaster coincided with an intensely cold spell. The Swanpool at Falmouth, was frozen over for example, enabling large numbers of people to enjoy the unusual pleasure of skating on it. Because of this bitter weather, a considerable number of persons - nine men, a boy and girl - were in the boiler house, with another man by the engine. About nine o'clock in the morning the boiler burst with a tremendous explosion. Nine of those in the building were so dreadfully injured by the concussion of steam, the scalding water and by the stones and bricks scattered in every direction that they died within a few hours,

CROSSCUT: A tunnel driven at right-angle to the main direction of the lodes. Driven to give access to parallel workings and to discover new lodes.

whilst two others were most severely injured.

An inquest was held at the account house the following day, when according to the gruesome custom of the time, the bodies of the victims were viewed by the jury before any evidence was taken.

Jane Goyne, a tin-dresser (bal-maiden) on the mine, described how she went with several other persons into the boiler house to warm herself about eight o'clock. After she had been there about five minutes, the engineman, James Sampson, asked her elder sister, Elizabeth, to fetch him a pitcher of water. Elizabeth refused, but Jane good-naturedly agreed to get it for him. She had left the boiler house less than half a minute when she heard a great noise and, looking back, saw steam ascending to a great height. Terrified, she ran off as fast as she could. She told the coroner how Elizabeth and others had been standing near the fireplace. She saw the engineman put coal on the fire and turn the gauge cocks to see that all was right, and then remain standing by them. Elizabeth, one may add, was among those killed in the explosion.

A miner, James Hocking, was in the engine house near the door leading to the boiler house when the boiler burst. He immediately pulled some clothes that were near him over his head. He was almost smothered by the steam and rubbish; when the rush of steam had subsided he looked about and saw two persons emerge from a large cupboard near him; one was hurt, but the other had escaped injury.

One of the mine captains, Richard James, was in the account house when the accident happened, and immediately went to give what help he could. He saw the victims taken out: 'All the deceased were dreadfully burnt and bruised; so much so, that their persons could scarcely be recognised; some were so scorched, that the skin of their hands fell off, and when picked up, was not unlike dry leather gloves.' The boiler had not been in use more than two or three days, after having undergone a thorough repair at the Redruth Hammer-mill. He could not account for the disaster but exonerated the engineman from all blame.

The victims of this dreadful accident included Sampson, the engineman; Elizabeth Goyne, the bal-maiden, aged about 20; a youth of fifteen; and six miners, several of whom left large families.

The blind miner of Botallack

One of the greatest dangers with which Cornish miners were beset in the old days was that of premature explosions; usually caused by the use of iron bars to ram home the gunpowder and tamping when preparing a hole for blasting. Iron will strike sparks from rock, and these are quite sufficient to ignite gunpowder, with usually tragic consequences to those standing nearby. Although it was known in

CROSSCOURSE: A geological fault which cuts across, often at right-angle, the main direction of the mineral-bearing lodes. They can vary from a few inches thick to several hundred metres, and sometimes can also contain valuable ores.

the second decade of the nineteenth century that the incidence of such mishaps could be greatly reduced by the substitution of copper-tipped instruments for iron bars, the indifference of mine agents and the gross carelessness of miners led to a continuance of explosions right up to the time when gunpowder was finally replaced by safer explosives towards the end of the century.

In these blasting accidents large numbers of men were killed outright; but many more were mangled or mutilated, the worst of these cases being of miners deprived of their sight. In days long prior to the advent of the Welfare State, these unfortunates found themselves in a truly pitiable situation. From being the breadwinner and chief support of a probably large family, they were reduced to receiving a miserably small pittance of a few shillings a week from the mine's sick or 'hurt' club - a dole that could terminate at a moment's notice on the closure of the mine. For the rest, there was only the charity of relatives and friends, eked out, perhaps by the possibility of hawking tea, bootlaces or other small articles from door to door with the assistance of a child to act as guide.

There is, however, on record one authentic case of a blinded miner continuing to work at his old employment despite the terrible and - one would think - well-nigh insuperable handicap with which he was afflicted. This instance occurred at Botallack, the celebrated submarine mine at St Just, whose ruined cliffside engine houses are among the most spectacular showpieces which Cornish industrial archaeology has to offer. This well-nigh incredible story is to be found in a little book, entitled *Cornwall: Its Mines and Miners* published in 1855. A labourer in this mine, he continued his perilous underground toil for a long period, from the dread of being compelled to accept parish relief. By these efforts he supported his family of nine children

and such was his marvellous recollection of every turning and winding of this subterranean temple of human industry, that he became a guide to his fellow-labourers, if by any accident their lights were extinguished! It is painful to add, that on being discharged from this employment (and they truly must have had rocky hearts who did discharge him) this poor blind man soon afterwards met his death in the following melancholy manner.

Pictured here is the Great Stull at the 412fm level of Dolcoath Mine. The photograph was taken in 1893, mere days before the disastrous collapse, which buried eight miners. Many of the pitch pine timber stull pieces were 33 feet (10 metres) long and were 20inches (0.5m) square. Note, the apparently chaotic state of the level, with men, materials, wagons and rocks everywhere. Appearances are deceptive, however, and the scene was typical of a busy level where ground was being opened up and ore removed as fast as possible. Whilst strengthening the stull, a catastrophic movement of thousands of tons of broken ground, stretching upwards for nearly 200 metres, caused the enormous timber supports to break. Of the eight men buried, only one was rescued after the heroic efforts of his mates. (RCM)

Being engaged as attendant to some bricklayers who were building a house at St Ives, it became part of his duty to carry the hods of mortar up to the scaffolding, from which, having taken a step too far back, he fell, and received such severe injury of the head that he almost immediately expired.

Catastrophic Collapses

One of the commonest causes of underground accidents has been the collapse of timbers erected to hold back previously broken waste rock. These were known as 'stulls', and they were constructed by placing enormous timbers, usually pitch-pine, across the bottom of stopes between the hanging and footwalls, at right-angles to the dip of the wallrock. They were then covered by smaller timbers to form a platform upon which waste rock could be thrown. These stulls served the dual purpose of saving the expense of hoisting unwanted stuff to surface and also of giving support to the hanging wall. Unfortunately, as older workings were abandoned and the miners moved deeper, the upper levels became choked with waste rock and debris, which was frequently anything but stable.

The timber stulls upon which much of this debris rested became rotten with time and constant wetting and drying as surface water inflow varied seasonally. At Dolcoath, the largest, deepest and one of the oldest continually working mines in Cornwall, some of the stull timbers in the upper levels were well over one-hundred years old. Records show that the problem of constantly moving waste rock and frequently collapsing stulls was the cause of daily worry at the old mine. In the 1820s there was great concern about the future of the mine when hundreds of thousands of tons of debris slowly moved downwards, closing tunnels and filling working stopes. Two dreadful accidents at Dolcoath serve to illustrate the extent of this ongoing problem.

In November 1872 five men were blasting rock on the 212fm level, west of Wheal Bryant Shaft. The blast disturbed loose ground nearby, which was supported on a stull. Fifteen metres below them a miner called Thomas Henry Borlase was standing on another stull, when he heard the crack and roar of moving ground and after shouting a warning to two boys working nearby, ran for his life. They, instinctively, ran beneath the stull upon which Borlase had stood, and were swept away as over 400 tons of loose rock smashed the half-metre thick timbers into matchwood. They were fifteen year old Simon Baston and sixteen year old William Henry Moffat. Below them, on the 224fm level, a miner called Thomas Oxnam, his two sons and two other miners heard the din and attempted to escape. The older of the Oxnam boys, grabbed his younger brother and ran to safety as did the other two miners, but the father of those two lads did not escape. He ran the wrong way. Immediately after the tragedy occurred, every miner on the level rushed to the scene and began digging. The first body found was that of William Moffat and it was most dreadfully crushed. Later Baston was dug out of the debris, but it was the next day before the rescuers found the body of Oxnam. He was six metres below the 224fm level and his head was crushed. Thomas Oxnam's older son, Thomas Henry, almost certainly saved the life of his brother, but it is a tragedy that Borlase's shouted warning might well have sent Baston and Moffat to their deaths.

On September 20th 1893, there occurred at Dolcoath possibly the worst accident to have happened in that mine's history. As Dolcoath's main lode went deeper it not only flattened out, but its width gradually grew greater. The eastern workings especially were very wide, and the distance between the foot and hanging walls at the 412 and 425fm levels, which were then the deepest levels at Dolcoath, was over 10 metres in places. The accident happened on the 412fm level at an extremely wide

excavation, which was supported by the 'great stull'. Following an inspection of this stull by the mine manager, Captain Josiah Thomas and the senior underground agent, Captain James Johns, it was decided that the timbers needed strengthening, as one of the stull timbers appeared to be showing stress.

This 'great stull' consisted of twenty-two pieces of half metre square, pitch-pine timbers, the average length of which was some 10 metres. They were set at an angle of 45 degrees, which was right-angled to the hanging wall. Below the stull were timbers set horizontally across the level to support the long stull pieces. Above it was another, smaller stull, and between these was packed debris. Above this, and extending upwards for a height of over 180 metres was a huge body of waste rock of varying stability. The 400fm level, a short distance above the stull, was actually driven through this enormous

STULL: Large timbers placed in the workings to support the hanging wall and to form platforms upon which waste rock could be thrown.

body of fairly loose rubble, and protected by timber.

After the inspection Captain Johns told the timbermen to insert into the stull two large pieces of half metre square pitch-pine, to strengthen it. The first piece was on the level and other was about to be sent down. The leading timberman, was called John Pollard, and his right-hand man was Charles White. They were assisted by at least fourteen others  as they struggled to place the extremely heavy stull piece in position. Apart from eleven miners, the gang included a boy and four Camborne School of Mine students. For the actual task the gang was split into two groups, one of which was working at the western end of the stull, nearest to the tunnel to New East Shaft, and the other group, supervised by Pollard and White, were engaged in installing the timber. The top end of the seven metre long timber had been lifted to the hanging wall, by the eight man crew, who were positioning it by means of a rope block. Suddenly, there was a 'God send' – a fall of gravel and rock, which can give a warning under such circumstances. About a ton

of debris fell and although the men were used to such occurrences, they all took this sign seriously and dashed for the tunnel at the end of the stull. Unfortunately, although the men at the eastern end were able to make it to safety, those directly beneath the centre of the stull stood no chance, as the initial warning was followed immediately by a cataclysmic roar as thousands of tons of rock and earth destroyed the entire massive stull and buried the eight miners beneath it.

The movement of air caused by this tremendous displacement of ground swept miners off their feet and literally hurled stones with great force along the level. Two miners were struck as they ran, and one boy, Jimmy Tresawna, was carried by the air current for a distance of seven metres. A stationary wagon, which was off track, was blown some five and half metres along the level, striking and injuring a miner. Men had their clothes blown off and others suffered a variety of injuries from the flying debris. Miners working hundreds of metres away from the scene heard the noise and wondered what tragedy had occurred. The survivors picked themselves up and went back to the collapse to investigate. They were faced by an impenetrable mass of rock, timber and rubbish. They called out, but received no reply. One man climbed up to the 400fm level, but found the level above the stull had been swept away by the massive movement of broken ground. The mass of rock some 180 metres high had shifted down and filled a large part of the mine with debris. Nonplussed, the survivors took the news to the surface, so that an organised rescue could be arranged. Gangs of miners then worked round the clock to tunnel in from both sides to reach the victims. It was a painfully slow business, as some of the fallen rock was extremely large and all the ground had to be supported by timber as they went. The men worked steadily on despite receiving no encouraging sounds from within the pile. Then, about three o'clock in the following afternoon, the gang tunnelling in from the eastern side, heard a voice calling: 'Praise the Lord!' The tunnellers, who had advanced over five metres into the pile, were delighted. William John Osborne, of Camborne, had been lying beneath the rock, his legs pinned by a piece of timber, 'praising the Lord' for over 26 hours. He told the rescuers, that he had heard no one else's voice whilst there. Two small miners were able to crawl through the pile for about ten metres toward Osborne, but could not get close enough to pass a tube to him for liquid food. It proved impossible to get to him before he died, but his courage and steadfastness inspired the miners to greater efforts. Just after 8 o'clock in the evening the men heard another voice inside the debris. It was Richard Davies of Troon, who was able to tell the tunnellers that he was unhurt, with no rock or timber on any part of him. He was then about nine metres from the eastern rescuers, and was able to crawl some distance toward them. One of the rescuers, called Smith, crawled through the tunnel towards Davies, and when he was close he reached out his hand to touch Davies and comfort him, but upon remarking how cold his hand was, was informed that both his hands were free. Smith had gripped the hand of a dead miner. Eventually, Smith was able to pass a hatchet through to Davies, who cut the hole wider and was able to wriggle through to safety. Davies tried to stand, but had to be supported. He was hauled up to the 400fm level and then taken by gig to the surface.

Richard Davies was the only survivor of those eight men

entombed there. The rescuers worked on, enduring not only tremendous difficulty and danger, but also having to suffer the appalling stench of the dead bodies. The last body, that of Charles White, was recovered almost three weeks after the accident, on October 9th. The dead men were, John Pollard, chief timberman, Charles White, senior timberman, William John Osborne, John Henry Jennings, Frederick John Harvey, James Adams and Richard James. Camborne was well used to mining accidents, but this was one of the worst the community ever had to suffer, and for the scores of miners involved in the rescue attempt, the experience was particularly harrowing.